DISCARD

Talking Hands

AT PLAY

EN EL JUEGO

WRITTEN BY KATHLEEN PETELINSEK AND E. RUSSELL PRIMM
ILLUSTRATED BY NICHOLE DAY DIGGINS

A SPECIAL THANKS TO OUR ADVISERS: JUNE PRUSAK IS A DEAF THERAPEUTIC RECREATOR WHO
BELIEVES IN THE MOTTO "LIFE IS GOOD," REGARDLESS OF YOUR ABILITY TO HEAR.

CARMINE L. VOZZOLO IS AN EDUCATOR WHO WORKS WITH CHILDREN
WHO ARE DEAF OR HARD OF HEARING AND THEIR FAMILIES.

Published in the United States of America by The Child's World®
PO Box 326, Chanhassen, MN 55317-0326
800-599-READ
www.childsworld.com

Cover / frontispiece: left, right—Photodisc.

Interior: 3, 5, 7, 12, 19, 20—RubberBall Productions; 4—Thinkstock / Punchstock; 6, 8, 9, 10, 11, 13, 14, 15, 16, 17, 18, 21—Photodisc; 22—Brand X Pictures; 23—Swerve / Alamy Images.

The Child's World®: Mary Berendes, Publishing Director

Editorial Directions, Inc.: E. Russell Primm, Editorial Director; Katie Marsico, Project Editor and Managing Editor; Caroline Wood, Editorial Assistant; Javier Millán, Proofreader; Cian Laughlin O'Day, Photo Researcher and Selector

The Design Lab: Kathleen Petelinsek, Art Director; Julia Goozen, Art Production

LIBRARY OF CONGRESS CATALOGING-IN-PUBLICATION DATA
Petelinsek, Kathleen.
    At play = En el juego / by Kathleen Petelinsek and E. Russell Primm.
        p. cm. — (Talking hands)
    Summary: Provides illustrations of American Sign Language signs and Spanish and English text for various games and sports.
    In English, Spanish, and American Sign Language.
    ISBN 1-59296-683-7 (lib. bdg. : alk. paper)
    1. American Sign Language—Vocabulary—Juvenile literature. 2. Spanish language—Vocabulary—Juvenile literature. 3. Sports—Juvenile literature. 4. Games—Juvenile literature. I. Primm, E. Russell, 1958– II. Title. III. Title: En el juego. IV. Series: Petelinsek, Kathleen. Talking hands.
    HV2476.P4713 2006
    419'.7083461–dc22   2006009037

NOTE TO PARENTS AND EDUCATORS:

The understanding of any language begins with the acquisition of vocabulary, whether the language is spoken or manual. The books in the Talking Hands series provide readers, both young and old, with a first introduction to basic American Sign Language signs. Combining close photo cues and simple, but detailed, line illustration, children and adults alike can begin the process of learning American Sign Language. In addition to the English word and sign for that word, we have included the Spanish word. The addition of the Spanish word is a wonderful way to allow children to see multiple ways (English, Spanish, signed) to say the same word. This is also beneficial for Spanish-speaking families to learn the sign even though they may not know the English word for that object.

Let these books be an introduction to the world of American Sign Language. Most languages have regional dialects and multiple ways of expressing the same thought. This is also true for sign language. We have attempted to use the most common version of the signs for the words in this series. As with any language, the best way to learn is to be taught in person by a frequent user. It is our hope that this series will pique your interest in sign language.

Baseball
Béisbol

1.

2.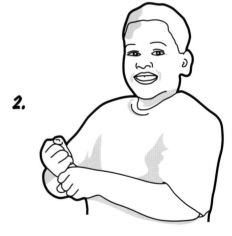

Both hands have closed fists. Move as if you are swinging a bat. Repeat.

Ambas manos hacen puños cerrados. Mover come si estuviera bateando. Repetir.

3

Frisbee
Frisbee

1.

2.

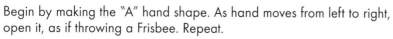

Begin by making the "A" hand shape. As hand moves from left to right, open it, as if throwing a Frisbee. Repeat.

Comience forando la "A" con la mano. Mover la mano de la izquierda a la derecha, abrirla, como si se estuviera lanzando el Frisbee. Repetir.

Jump Rope
Cuerda de Saltar

1.

Both hands make the "A" hand shape and move in a circular motion.

Ambas manos forman la "A" y se mueven en forma circular.

5

Tennis
Tenis

1.

2.

Move right arm across and back, as if you are swinging a tennis racket.

Mover el brazo derecho hacia el frente y hacia atrás, como si estuviera oscilando la raqueta de tenis.

6

Soccer
Fútbol

1.

2.

Move right hand into palm of left hand. Repeat.

Mover la mano derecha y poner debajo de la palma de la mano izquierda. Repetir.

Rock Climbing
Alpinismo

1.

2.

1) Right fist taps top of left fist. 2) Curl fingers of both hands. Alternate hands moving up and down.

1) El puño derecho golpetea ligeramente la parte superior de la mano izquierda. 2) Enrosque los dedos de ambas manos. Alterna las manos moviendo para arriba y para abajo.

Skiing
Esquí

1.

Both hands make the "X" hand shape (with index fingertips pointing up). Right hand stays in front of left hand as both move down and away from body at the same time.

Ambas manos forman la "X" (las yemas de los dedos índices señalan hacia arriba). La mano derecha se mantiene al frente de la mano izquierda a medida que ambas se mueven hacia abajo y se alejan del cuerpo a la misma vez.

9

Golf Golf

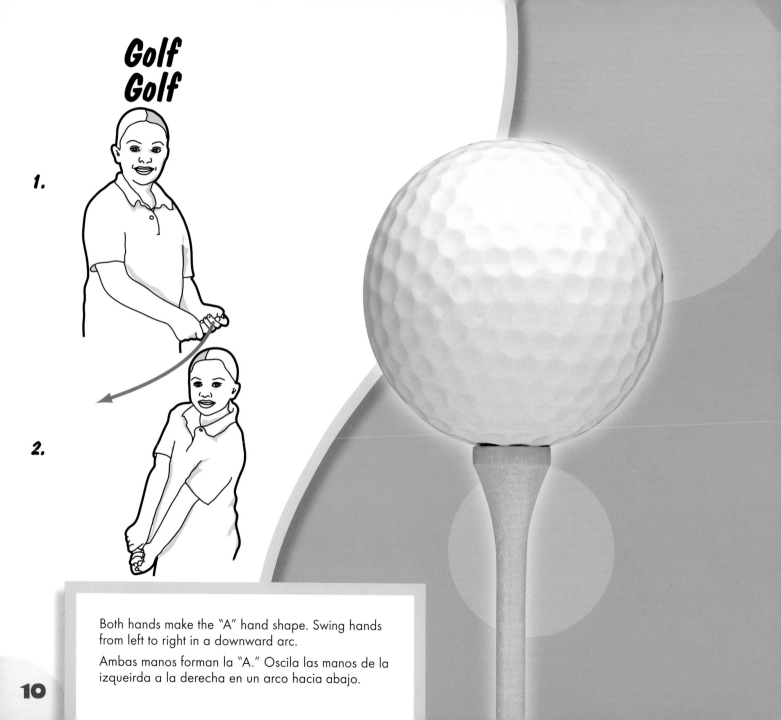

1.

2.

Both hands make the "A" hand shape. Swing hands from left to right in a downward arc.

Ambas manos forman la "A." Oscila las manos de la izqueirda a la derecha en un arco hacia abajo.

10

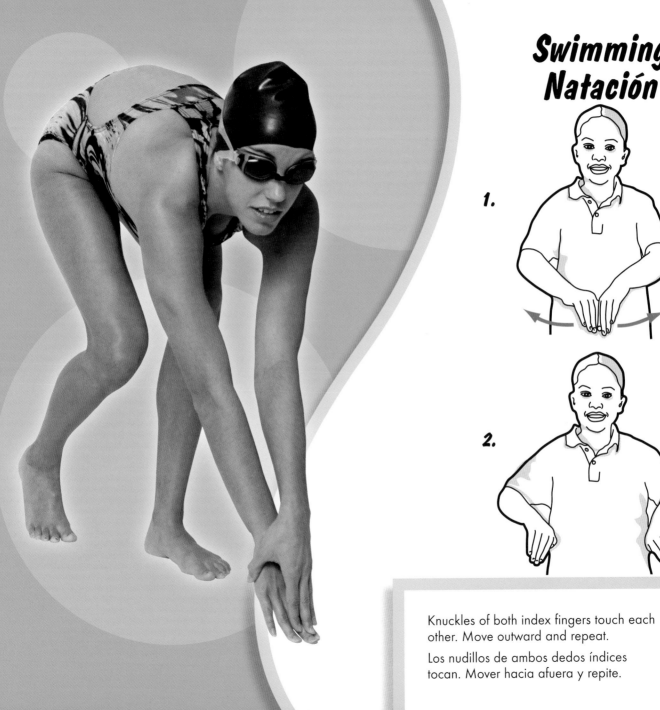

Swimming
Natación

1.

2.

Knuckles of both index fingers touch each other. Move outward and repeat.

Los nudillos de ambos dedos índices tocan. Mover hacia afuera y repite.

Volleyball
Voleibol

1.

2.

Touch tips of middle fingers to thumbs.
Flick. Repeat.

Tocar las yemas de los dedos medios con
los pulgares. Sacudir. Repetir.

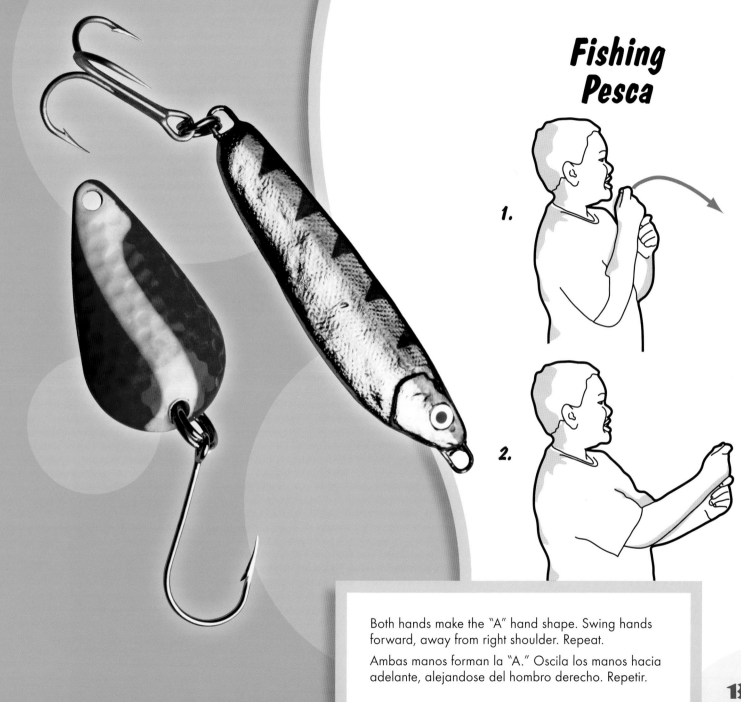

Fishing
Pesca

1.

2.

Both hands make the "A" hand shape. Swing hands forward, away from right shoulder. Repeat.

Ambas manos forman la "A." Oscila los manos hacia adelante, alejandose del hombro derecho. Repetir.

Boxing
Boxeo

1.

Rotate both fists up and away from chest in a circular motion.

Girar ambos puños hacia arriba y alejar del pecho en forma circular.

Skateboarding
Patineta

1.

Right index and middle fingers touch top of flat left hand (palm down) as both hands move back and forth together.

El dedo índice derecho y el dedo medio tocan la parte superior de la mano izquierda (palma hacia abajo) ambas manos se mueven hacia adelante y hacia atrás.

Ice Skating
Patinaje de Hielo

1.

2.

Both hands make the "X" hand shape (with index fingers pointing up). As one hand moves away from body, the other moves toward body. Repeat.

Ambas manos forman la "X" (los dedos índices señalan hacia arriba). A medida que una mano se aleja del cuerpo y la otra se mueve hacia el cuerpo. Repetir.

Bowling
Bolos

1.

2.

Curl fingers of right hand. Bring right arm forward and slightly upward.

Enrosque los dedos de la mano derecha. Mover el brazo derecho hacia adelante y ligeramente hacia arriba.

Bike Riding
Ciclismo

1.

Rotate both fists up and away from
stomach area in a circular motion. Repeat.

Oscila ambos puños hacia arriba y alejar
del estómago en forma circular. Repetir.

Lacrosse
Vilorta

1.

2.

Swing fists from right shoulder to left shoulder. Repeat.

Gire los puños desde el hombro derecho hasta el hombro izquierdo. Repetir.

Game
Juego

1.

2.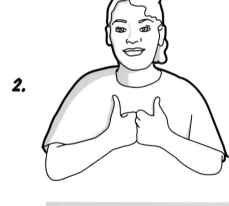

Both fists (with thumbs out) tap knuckles. Repeat.

Ambos puños (con los pulgares hacia afuera) tocan los nudillos. Repetir.

Win
Ganar

1.

2.

3.

Hands close in fists as they move inward. Bottom of right fist touches top of left fist. Left hand stays still while right hand continues to move to left side of body.

Ambas manos forman puños a medida que se mueven hacia adentro. La parte inferior del puño derecho toca la parte superior del puño izquierdo. La mano izquierda se mantiene immóvil mientras que la mano derecha sigue moviéndose al lado izquierdo del cuerpo.

Lose
Perder

1.

2.

Right hand makes the "V" hand shape and moves down to left palm (which does not move).

La mano derecha forma la "V" y se mueve hacia abajo de la palma izquierda (la mano izquierda no se mueve).

Tie
Empatar

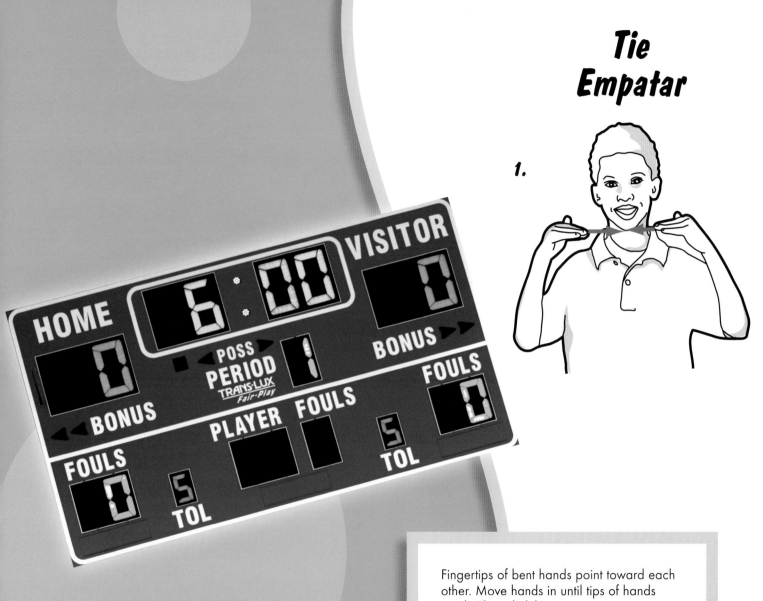

1.

Fingertips of bent hands point toward each other. Move hands in until tips of hands touch. Then slightly separate.

Las yemas de los dedos en forma de garra frente a frente. Mover las manos hasta que las yemas de los dedos se juntan. Separa los dedos ligeramente.

A B C D E F
G H I J K
L M N O P
Q R S T U
V W X Y Z

Alina is seven years old and is in the second grade. Her favorite things to do are art, soccer, and swimming. DJ is her brother!

Dareous has seven brothers and sisters. He likes football. His favorite team is the Detroit Lions. He also likes to play with his Gameboy and Playstation.

DJ is eight years old and is in the third grade. He loves playing the harmonica and his Gameboy. Alina is his sister!

24